D1537356

MEXICO
Leading the Southern Hemisphere

VICTORIA!
THE SPORTS OF MEXICO

MC MASON CREST
PHILADELPHIA

Mexican soccer star Javier "El Chicharito" Hernandez in action with the Mexican national team. In 2011 he was the most valuable player in the CONCACAF Gold Cup tournament.

MEXICO
Leading the Southern Hemisphere

VICTORIA!
THE SPORTS OF MEXICO

MASON CREST
PHILADELPHIA

Mason Crest
450 Parkway Drive, Suite D
Broomall, PA 19008
www.masoncrest.com

Printed and bound in the United States of America.

CPSIA Compliance Information: Batch #M2014.
For further information, contact Mason Crest at 1-866-MCP-Book.

First printing

1 3 5 7 9 8 6 4 2

Library of Congress Cataloging-in-Publication Data
on file at the Library of Congress

ISBN: 978-1-4222-3220-0 (hc)
ISBN: 978-1-4222-8685-2 (ebook)

Mexico: Leading the Southern Hemisphere series ISBN: 978-1-4222-3213-2

TABLE OF CONTENTS

MEXICO

Leading the Southern Hemisphere

KEY ICONS TO LOOK FOR:

 Text-dependent questions: These questions send the reader back to the text for more careful attention to the evidence presented there.

 Words to understand: These words with their easy-to-understand definitions will increase the reader's understanding of the text, while building vocabulary skills.

 Series glossary of key terms: This back-of-the book glossary contains terminology used throughout this series. Words found here increase the reader's ability to read and comprehend higher-level books and articles in this field.

 Research projects: Readers are pointed toward areas of further inquiry connected to each chapter. Suggestions are provided for projects that encourage deeper research and analysis.

 Sidebars: This boxed material within the main text allows readers to build knowledge, gain insights, explore possibilities, and broaden their perspectives by weaving together additional information to provide realistic and holistic perspectives.

TIMELINE

1000 B.C.	A form of Mesoamerican ballgame is developed by the Olmec civilization; this game is later played by the Toltecs, Maya, Aztecs, and others.
1800s	Soccer is introduced in Mexico; rodeos become popular.
1890s	Baseball is first played in Mexico.
1902	The first amateur soccer league begins with five teams.
1910	The Mexican Revolution begins.
1921	With the end of the Mexican Revolution, baseball spreads throughout Mexico; the Asociación Nacional de Charros is formed.
1928	Mexico's first jai alai court opens in Mexico City.
1929	Mexico joins the Fédération Internationale de Football Association (FIFA).
1930	Mexico plays in the first FIFA World Cup game.
1933	Federación Nacional de Charros is developed to regulate charro groups.
1936	Mexico's basketball team takes the bronze medal at the Olympic games.
1948	Horseback riders win Mexico's first gold medals. The historic events were individual and team showjumping.
1955	The Mexican League, a professional baseball league, is formed.
1960	The Mexican Central League is formed.
1968	Two boxers win gold medals at the Olympics: Antonio Roldán wins in the featherweight category and Ricardo Delgado wins in the flyweight.

8

1970   Manuel Raga becomes the first Mexican-born player to be drafted by the NBA; he plays for the Hawks; Mexico hosts the World Cup finals.

1981   Rookie Fernando Valenzuela wins the National League's Cy Young Award, the first Mexican-born pitcher to do so. Valenzuela would win 173 games during his major-league career.

1984   José Manuel Youshimatz wins Mexico's only Olympic medal in cycling; he takes the bronze in the 50-kilometer race.

1986   Jorge Campos signs on with UNAM (Pumas); Mexico again hosts the World Cup finals.

1995   The first Mexican National One-Wall Championships are held in Guadalupe.

1999   Adriana Fernández becomes the first Mexican woman to win the New York City Marathon; she is the first woman of Mexico to accomplish this feat.

2000   Soraya Jiménez lifts her way to the gold medal podium at the Sydney Olympics.

2004   Four Mexican athletes win medals at the Olympic Games in Athens: Ana Guevara (silver, 400m), Belem Guerrero (silver, cycling), Oscar Salazar (silver, Taekwondo), and Iridia Salazar (bronze, Taekwondo).

2010   Professional golfer Lorena Ochoa retires from the sport after spending three years as the world's top-ranked female golfer.

2012   The Mexican fútbol team defeats Brazil to win the Olympic gold medal. Overall, Mexican athletes win seven medals at the games.

2014   Mexico competes in the 2014 World Cup in Brazil.

9

WORDS TO UNDERSTAND

amateurs—people who engage in sport for recreation rather than pay.

arena—an enclosed area used for public entertainment.

contact sport—a game that involves physical contact between contestants.

recruit—to enlist new members for a team.

scout—a person who look for new talent for a sports team.

umpire—the official who ensures that the rules are obeyed during a game.

Members of Mexico's national soccer team huddle before an international match. Soccer (fútbol) is wildly popular in Mexico.

TEAM SPORTS ARE TOPS IN MEXICO

The favorite sport of the people of Mexico is soccer, which they call *fútbol*. Children and adults play this game in different **leagues**, while professional players can participate in various competitions. Of course, **amateurs** can play in many soccer leagues throughout Mexico. Or they can even play in the comfort of their own backyards.

The history of soccer may be traced back to the first people of Mexico. The original inhabitants of Mesoamerica played a ballgame that resembled modern-day soccer in some ways. Their version involved a large ball and goals. Players from both teams used their hips to move the balls and score goals. Like in today's sport, players could not use their hands to touch the ball. However, after games, the losers did not exactly shake hands with the winners. Archaeologists believe that these games often ended with members of the losing team being sacrificed as part of a ritual to appease the local deities!

During the 19th century, Europeans introduced their version of soccer to Mexico. Today, soccer is the most popular sport in Latin America. It is believed that one of the first national soccer leagues in Mexico was formed around 1903.

Dario Carreno of Monterrey (left) and Manuel Lopez of Puebla battle for the ball in a Liga MX match, the highest level of professional soccer in Mexico.

By 1927, an association devoted to *fútbol* had popped up. Mexico joined the Fédération Internationale de Football Association (FIFA), the international governing body for the sport, in 1929. Every four years, FIFA organizes the World Cup, a tournament of national teams that is the single most important event in the soccer world. Mexico's national team has qualified for fourteen World Cups, most recently the 2014 event. However, the farthest the team has ever advanced in the tournament was reaching the quarterfinals, which it did in both 1970 and

1986. Both of those years, Mexico was the host nation for the World Cup, meaning all the final games were played there.

Mexico's greatest international soccer accomplishment came in 2012, when the national team won the gold medal at the Olympic Games. Mexico won its pool, then defeated Senegal and Japan to reach the finals. In the championship, the Mexican team defeated powerful Brazil by a 2-1 score. Both of Mexico's goals were scored by Oribe Peralta.

There is a professional soccer league in Mexico, known as Liga MX. The most successful teams include Club de Fútbol América S.A and Club Deportivo Guadalajara, which have each won 11 league titles. Deportivo Toluca Fútbol Club S.A., from the state of Mexico, has won 10 titles.

One reason that soccer is popular in Mexico is because the sport can be played virtually anywhere with any equipment. A person can practice the

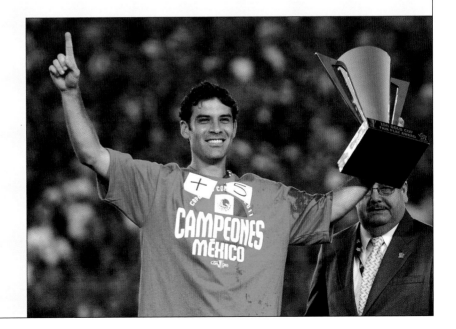

Rafael Marquez celebrates Mexico's victory over the United States in the 2011 CONCACAF Gold Cup, a prestigious tournament. Marquez was captain of Mexico's national team during the 2010 and 2014 World Cup tournaments.

13

14

sport alone, or pick up teams with nearly any number of players. There is no special court or field required, and even the ball doesn't have to be regulation—a scrunched up rag wrapped with tape can do in a pinch!

Women also play soccer in Mexico. In 1999 a Mexican team qualified for the Women's World Cup tournament for the first time. Even though the team was eliminated from the tournament without winning a game, its presence in the World Cup led to the start of a women's soccer program. One of Mexico's greatest soccer coaches, Leonardo Cuéllar, has helped the development of women' soccer in the country.

People of te United States, Mexico's neighbor to the north, has loved baseball for years. But Mexicans also enjoy baseball—or *béisbol*, as they call it. The people of the Yucatán peninsula—called Yucatecos—really like the sport. They call baseball "*el rey de los deportes*"—the king of sports.

Some say baseball may even have first originated in Mexico. Certainly, Yucatán was one of several regions where the game was first played in the early 1890s, but most historians think that Cubans were responsible for bringing baseball to Mexico. During the Spanish-American War, islanders left Cuba to get away from the fighting. Baseball was already a favorite sport on Cuba, and when they came to Mexico, they kept playing.

In Mexico, the new game soon caught on. Young men and boys began playing baseball in streets and alleyways. These games were not formal, of course. In fact, most players didn't even wear shoes. Pitchers wore no gloves. Players made bats out of sticks, boards, and pipes. Wadded up rags could be used as balls.

The first great baseball player to come from Mexico was a man named Bobby Ávila. In the 1950s, he played for the Cleveland Indians. Later he took up politics in Mexico.

More than 110 Mexicans have played Major League Baseball in the United States. One of them is pitcher Rodrigo Lopez, pictured here on the mound for the Philadelphia Phillies in 2009.

15

Bases could be anything that marked a place. *Umpires* rarely wore masks.

Mérida's and Progreso's real baseball teams were formed in 1892. Later, baseball parks were built. Men from wealthy families learned how to play baseball abroad, and when these men came back to Mexico, they played in the team called the Sporting Club. Baseball grew more popular, but when the economy slumped in the late 1890s, baseball's growth came to a stop.

But things picked up in again with the turn of the century. Villages set up clubs for people to play baseball. Players paid dues so they could use equipment.

Wealthy men who could afford regulation gloves, bats, and balls could play in two elite teams: El Trovador, which began in 1901, and the Pablo Gonzalez Baseball Club. You didn't have to be a member of the wealthy upper class to play baseball, however; men who worked for a living could also play on the El Fénix, Railway, and Club Colón teams. Financial problems again stopped baseball's growth in 1905.

Interest in baseball did not spread throughout Mexico until the 1920s, after the Revolution. Men of different backgrounds now played in towns and villages. And this time, baseball had come to stay.

In 1925, the Mexican League was formed. In 15 years this league became the major professional league for baseball in Mexico. In 1946 Jorge Pasquel, the commissioner of the Mexican League, even started inviting players from the United States to come and play ball for his teams. Today, the Mexican League has 16 teams, with the quality of play considered roughly equal to that of a AAA team in the American minor leagues.

Scouts from the United States do attend Mexican League games, and *recruit* players for the major leagues. Since the 1980s, some of baseball's biggest stars, like pitcher Fernando Valenzuela, have been from Mexico. In 1981, as a rookie for the Los Angeles Dodgers, Valenzuela became the first Mexican-born pitcher to win the National League Cy Young Award, which is given to the best pitcher each season. Another Mexican ballplayer who became star is outfielder Vinny Castilla, who hit 320 home runs during his 16-year MLB career. Some successful Mexican players today include pitchers Yovani Gallardo and Jaime Garcia.

Mexicans enjoy playing and watching baseball. Kids can play in little league games, while adults often play on local teams. Entrance to professional games is relatively inexpensive, and many people who can't get to ball games watch this fun sport on television. In the warmer areas of Mexico, baseball is played all year round.

Informal baseball games in village plazas are common in Mexico. Baseball, soccer, and basketball are all popular among young people in part because they can be played nearly anywhere and require very little equipment.

Eduardo Nájera averaged about 5 points and 4 rebounds per game during his NBA career. He played for the Dallas Mavericks (2000–2004; 2010), the Golden State Warriors (2004–2005), the Denver Nuggets (2005–2008), the New Jersey Nets (2008–2010), and the Charlotte Bobcats (2010–2012).

Basketball is another popular team sport in Mexico. In 1936, the Mexican basketball team went to the Olympics and brought back a bronze medal. Basketball is still popular in today's Mexico. A professional basketball league, the Liga Nacional de Baloncesto Profesional (LNBP) was founded in 2000. Today, it has 16 teams and is one of the strongest basketball leagues in Latin America.

Many basketball fans also follow American NBA teams, such as the San Antonio Spurs, Phoenix Suns, and Dallas Mavericks. Two Mexican athletes have played in the NBA. Horacio Llamas was the first Mexican to play for an NBA team, the Phoenix Suns, in 1996. He played several seasons, then competed in the Mexican Basketball League until 2013. Eduardo Nájera was drafted in 2000 by the Mavericks and played 12 seasons in the NBA.

Some Mexicans also play American football, which they call *fútbol Americano*. In recent years a college football league has emerged, with Águilas Blancas being one of the most successful of these teams. Águilas Blancas has won the college championship of *fútbol Americano* five times.

The popularity of this sport continues to grow, but for many Mexicans, *fútbol Americano* is too expensive to play, as schools and clubs cannot afford the equipment and insurance required. However, even if they cannot play *fútbol Americano* themselves, Mexicans are still interested in the sport. Cities like Monterrey, Nuevo León, and Mexico City have hosted pre-season NFL games, and in 2005 more than 103,000 people came to Mexico City's Aztec Stadium to watch the Arizona Cardinals defeat the San Francisco 49ers in the first regular-season NFL game played outside the United States.

TEXT-DEPENDENT QUESTIONS

In what years did Mexico host the World Cup finals?

What do people who live on the Yucatán Peninsula call béisbol?

RESEARCH PROJECT

Look at the roster of Mexico's 2014 World Cup team (it is available at FIFA's official site, http://www.fifa.com/worldcup/teams/team=43911/players.html). Choose a player, and find out more about him. Where was he born? When did he start playing soccer? Has he played professionally, and if so for which teams? Write a one-page report about the player and present it to the class, along with photos of him in action.

Words to Understand

laxative—a drug that loosens bowel movements and may cause diarrhea.

rodeo—a public performance that involves bronco riding, calf roping, steer wrestling, and bull riding.

stud—a male animal used for breeding because of its good bloodlines, championship pedigree, or desirable characteristics.

tranquilizers—drugs used to calm or sedate.

The largest bullfighting stadium in the world is the
Plaza de Toros in Mexico City. The stadium, which
opened in 1946, can hold more than 60,000 people.

ANIMAL SPORTS
TRADITION OR CRUELTY?

The Spanish term for bullfighting is *corrida de toros*, and the Spaniards were the ones who developed this sport. They brought bullfighting to Mexico when they first arrived in the 1500s. Today, Mexico is home to more than 200 arenas for bullfighting. In fact, the biggest bullring in the world is located in Mexico City. The stadium, the Plaza de Toros de México, holds 50,000 spectators.

As its name suggests, the object of this sport is to fight a bull...and survive. The person who attempts this task is called a *matador*. Mexicans treat these bullfighters like stars. Little boys pretend to be these national heroes.

Since an average man may weigh 160 pounds while a bull may weigh over 1,000 pounds, successful matadors must show great intelligence and bravery inside the ring. Being a

If the crowd thinks a matador gave a wonderful show then the president of the bullring can award the bullfighter with the bull's ears or tail. One ear is cut off and given for a great show. Two ears are given for a grand performance. But for an unforgettable event, two ears and a tail are awarded to the matador.

21

matador is dangerous: one in four is crippled, and one in ten is killed during a bullfight. When bulls become enraged they may gore the bullfighter with their horns. On average, each matador gets gored about once during a six-month season.

Despite the danger he faces, the matador takes great pride in dressing for the big event. He wears an ornate costume called a *traje de luces*. This "suit of lights" can cost thousands of dollars. It consists mainly of a jacket, tight pants, vest, and a hat, all very fancy. They may have silver and gold accents all over for full effect. The outfit's final touch is the crimson red cape. This cape is sometimes draped over the matador's shoulders at the start of the performance. Later, the cape can be waved around to annoy the bulls.

These enormous creatures are not regular cattle. They are *toros de lidia*, fighting bulls bred specifically for bullfighting. Through the years, these bulls have developed a natural tendency to charge. They are more hostile than ordinary bulls.

Most Mexican bullfights take place on Sunday afternoons. Shows may have as many as six bulls lined up for fights. The event begins with rhythmic music playing throughout the stands. Dancing and parades are common too. A greased pig chase or a **rodeo** can be added for the audience's enjoyment. Once these festivities cease, the ground is cleared for the main event.

A bull is set free from his *toril* or pen. He usually arrives in the arena angry. A beginning matador waves his cape around to excite the bull. Now comes a *picador*. This person rides a horse into the ring. He wears a beige hat called a *castoreno*. He also wears knight-like armor on his legs for protection. He carries at least one lance called a *pica* or *vara*. This lance has a steel point to spear the bull's neck and shoulder area. The maneuver makes the bull lower his head to

During a bullfight, the bull is first weakened by being stuck with short barbed lances, which are thrust into its shoulders and left hanging. The matador then uses a cape to move the bull around the ring, tiring it out, before moving in and using a sword to kill the animal.

24

A matador's cape is an essential dramatic element of the sport. More of a psychological threat than a physical one, the matador uses it to excite the bull as well as the crowd.

anticipate the kill. After the bull is lanced, come the *banderilleros*.

The banderilleros, usually three, run up to the bull. They carry brightly colored, sharp sticks called *banderillas*. They poke these sticks into the bull's back. After charging the picador's horse, a bull can be tired, and the banderilleros' job is to enliven it for the final part of the bullfight. The bull may now have been viciously stabbed up to six times. When he is in agonizing pain, he finally meets the real matador.

A bullfighter has only a few minutes of fame: he must kill the bull within 10 minutes of his entrance. His first maneuver is to add to the bull's fury by waving the red cape. The bull charges the matador, and the matador uses catlike movements to escape the sharp horns. The footwork of the bullfighter may be quite graceful and look like a dance with death. After several passes, the matador prepares for the kill. He takes out his sword, called an *estoque*.

The matador approaches the exhausted bull. The creature's head is bent down as it submits to the inevitable. The bullfighter thrusts his sword in between the bull's shoulder blades. This move is called the *estocada*. If the bull is still standing, another blade called a *descabello* is used. This sword cuts the spinal cord in the bull's neck. Once the bull is on the ground, a banderillero will spear the bull one last time with a *puntilla*, a small knife. This action signals the end of the bullfight. Onlookers shout "*Olé!*" when they like a move or when the bull is killed.

If the crowd feels that the bull was especially brave, they cheer for the president of the bullring to let the bull take a *vuelta*, a circle around the arena. A vuelta makes the bull's breeder very

Bulls do not get mad at the color red. They are actually color-blind. What enrages bulls are moving objects. So they charge at the cape because it moves, not because it is red.

25

proud and honored. Horses drag the dead bull around the ring to the sound of applause. Finally, the bull's body is pulled out of the arena by the horses. Butchers then cut up the animal and sell the beef.

Can a bull ever enter a bullring and live to tell about it? In rare instances, yes. If a bull has shown exceptional bravery and the crowd petitions the president of the bullring before it is killed, the president will grant an *indulto* (pardon) and spare the bull's life. The matador then pretends to kill the bull with a banderilla. Bulls who are spared usually go on to become **stud** bulls.

Many Mexicans also delight in rooster fights. This "sport" is called cockfighting, and the Spaniards were the ones who brought this form of entertainment to Mexico. During a cockfight, people sit around a dirt pit and place bets. Spectators guess which bird will die first. Cockfighting can bring in many pesos for winning owners.

To prepare for the fight, handlers tie metal spurs to one leg of each bird. Two roosters are put into the pit. The birds lunge and peck at one another, and the spurs can cause vicious wounds. If one of the birds grows weak, the other may peck at its head. If a time out is called, the handlers hit the birds to get their attention or they may enrage the roosters by plucking their feathers. By the time the birds are back in the ring again, they are furious. When beaks and claws attack, only one bird will live.

Sports like these may seem cruel and bloody to Americans, but they are a part of the Mexican culture. Many Mexicans agree that the sport of bullfighting is rich in culture and high in drama. Some see it as an art form that brings honor to both the country and the matadors. But more and more people are becoming disgusted with the cruelty of bullfighting. The sport takes place to bring in money from advertising sales, tickets, and beef, but

A group of people watch a cockfight, another popular animal sport in Mexico. Animal rights supporters have questioned the ethics of a tradition that calls for two birds to fight to the death for entertainment purposes. However, nearly every major Mexican city has an arena, called a *palenque*, where cockfights are held.

The bullfight often ends with a bull dead in the ring. Today, a growing number of people have called for the sport to be banned, as they view it as cruel to animals.

those who oppose bullfighting say that the profits do not justify the sport's cruelty. The bull is not given a chance, so it is not really a bull "fight" but merely a bull death.

Some people have said that bulls are intentionally debilitated before a fight. They are given tranquilizers and *laxatives* to weaken them or slow their reactions. Sometimes they are beaten, petroleum jelly is rubbed into their eyes to blur their vision, or they are confined in darkness for hours before being released into the bright arena. Some believe that the bull is often still conscious while his ears and tail are cut off. Bulls are usually stabbed several times in the lungs, because the matador frequently misses the heart. Baby bullfights, or *novilladas,* are even worse; no professional matador enters this arena, but instead, amateurs stab a calf to death. In recent years, an anti-bullfight campaign has developed and opposition to the sport is growing. However, bullfighting remains an important part of Mexican culture.

TEXT-DEPENDENT QUESTIONS
What is the world's largest bullfighting arena called? Where is it located?
How do gamecock handlers enrage their birds to make them fight?

RESEARCH PROJECT
Go to YouTube and look for videos of bullfights (one example can be found at https://www.youtube.com/watch?v=bPAkLjWgCHg). Once you watch the fight, do some more research on the pros and cons of bullfighting, and decide for yourself whether bullfights are good entertainment or animal cruelty. Write a short one-page essay that presents your conclusion on the matter, using facts to support your opinion.

 WORDS TO UNDERSTAND

meets—competitive events that draw a lot of athletes.

rappeler—a person who descends down a cliff while suspended from a rope.

A windsurfer glides across the sparkling water near Cabo San Lucas. Mexico is known for water and adventure sports that are challenging, fun, and conducted in picturesque locales.

WATER AND ADVENTURE SPORTS

Thousands of miles of coastlands plus rivers and lakes make Mexico one big water park. The country's mountains and canyons are great ground for backpacking. Ocean waves attract surfers and body boarders. People can look at fish as they snorkel or scuba dive. Or they can catch fish in one of the many seas or lakes. Swimming is a popular activity too.

Many Mexicans enjoy the thrill of surfing. This water sport is especially popular on the west side of the country, the part of Mexico that borders the Pacific Ocean. The areas to surf are plenty, including Boca de Pascuales, Michoacán, and Playa Linda. Boca de Pascuales is a surfer's dream—or nightmare; it's a rivermouth beach that has some of the biggest and fastest waves in Mexico.

The most well known beaches for catching a wave are at Zicatela Beach in Puerto Escondido. This surfing spot hosts so many great waves that it is called the Mexican Pipeline. It is ranked as one of the top surfing destinations in the world. Mexican and other surfers participate in competitions held there each year. Contests include the Mexpipe August Open, the Longboard Invitational,

Tourists come from across the globe to see the cliff divers of Acapulco. These clavadistas perform for crowds at La Quebrada. They dive from cliffs as high as 125 feet (35 meters) into a rough sea.

and the International Surfing Tournament. These events are usually held in the mid- to late summer and early fall.

Many miles of shorelines and lagoons invite swimming. But inland Mexicans may be landlocked, far from lakes and rivers. Since much of Mexico struggles with poverty, pools may be hard to find outside bigger cities. However, many Mexicans practice this sport. Some compete in *meets* from the regional to international levels.

The beauty beneath the sea beckons divers, and snorkeling and scuba diving interest coastal residents of Mexico. Palancar Reef off Cozumel features a

A scuba diver examines the undersea plant life in Cancún. Mexico has become a popular tourist spot in recent years, due in part to scuba diving and other recreational sports.

Fernando Platas of Mexico holds up the silver medal he won for diving at the 2000 Olympics.

collection of coral in a horseshoe formation. Parrot, angle, and butterfly fish come in outrageous colors that delight any diver. The Sea of Cortés offers a chance to swim with whale sharks. Divers can also go to Guerrero Negro's grey whale park. From January to early March, they can watch the California grey whales before they migrate.

Mexico's fishing industry is an important part of the nation's economy, but what is born of necessity can turn into fun. For some, fishing offers a relaxing time to get back to nature. For others, fishing can be a wild adventure. Deep-sea fishing can bring in a wide array of fish, depending on where it is done. The Yucatán Peninsula boasts bonefish, tarpon, snook, jacks, and barracuda. Just

Andres Sierra of Mexico competes in the canoe slalom event during the 2008 Olympic Trials. It is an intense sport, in which the canoist attempts to navigate his or her craft through a marked course on rough river water in the fastest time possible.

off the Baja Peninsula, fisherman can catch blue marlin, dorado, sailfish, tuna, amber jack, or even giant squid.

The adventure sports of Mexico get many hearts pumping. Some popular ways to get an adrenaline rush include kayaking and whitewater rafting. Rivers like Río Filos, Río Bobos, and Río Antigua combine beauty with excitement. The country's hills and mountains also entice *rappelers* and mountain climbers alike. Backpacking and camping are a way for nature lovers to catch a glimpse of the wild Mexico, which may be hidden from plain view.

Mexico has nearly 60 national parks and biosphere reserves. These offer everything from volcanoes to caverns, beaches to forests, abundant wildlife to blistering deserts. Because of the land's rich variety, Mexico is a wonderful place to explore—whether by land or water.

TEXT-DEPENDENT QUESTIONS

What areas of Mexico are popular among surfers?

Where is the Palancar reef located?

RESEARCH PROJECT

Using the Internet or your school library, find out about the sort of creatures that inhabit the barrier reefs off the Atlantic coast of Mexico, which are popular with divers. Choose one one of these sea creatures, and write a short report about it. Tell what the animal looks like, whether it is dangerous, what it eats, and how it survives and reproduces in the reef. Find photos online to include with your report, and present it to the class.

WORDS TO UNDERSTAND

fiestas—Spanish parties or celebrations.

haciendas—large Mexican estates or plantations.

mariachi—a type of music played by Mexican street bands.

A determined charro, or Mexican cowboy, does his best to stay on a bucking bull at a charrería. Rodeo animals are often poked and prodded to make them more aggressive, and therefore challenging to control.

MEXICANS RIDE 'EM, ROPE 'EM, AND WRANGLE 'EM

Mexicans sometimes refer to their version of the rodeo—the *charrería*—as their only national sport. This activity is so popular that participants are mentioned in the national anthem of Mexico. *Charros*—a type of cowboy—also participate in local parades, and each year they hold a place of honor in the country's September 16 Independence Day parade. Mexico even appointed a special day to honor the sport. September 14 is Charro Day.

This popular activity goes all the way back to the 1500s. The conquistadors of Spain created many of the events of today's Mexican rodeo. These Europeans also brought a main attraction of the rodeo—the horse.

Ever heard the line "get along, little dogie"? Cowboys called a calf with no mother a *dogie*. The term came from the Spanish word *dogal*, meaning a short rope used to keep a calf away from its mother while she was being milked.

Native Americans had never even seen a horse or cow until the Spaniards arrived.

Rodeos in Mexico started in Los Llanos de Apan, Hidalgo, where catching bulls by the tail was begun as a sport by Mexican cowboys called *vaqueros*. Shows involving horses and livestock had become well known by the 1800s. Whenever ranchers branded their cattle or rounded them up, they turned the events into great fun. People began traveling long distances to participate or watch the cowboys do their work. Contests developed, and charros would compete to see who handled the livestock the best. Large *fiestas* allowed the cowboys to display their great skill.

With the onset of the Mexican Revolution, many of the large *haciendas* were split up. To keep the charrería tradition alive, charros met in Mexico City. On July 4, 1921, the Asociación Nacional de Charros was born. This association made the rodeo a national sport of Mexico. And in 1933, the Federación Nacional de Charros was founded. This agency set the rules for regional charro groups. The federation gives the okay to people who want to host or participate in Mexican rodeos.

During the 1920s the charrería began changing, so that it was no longer simply a rodeo. Although rodeos and charrería are similar, a few major differences now exist between these two activities. Rodeo is an individual sport—that is to say each contestant competes separately in the events. In charrería, however, teams compete against each other. Another difference is that people who compete in a rodeo can earn cash prizes, while charros do not earn money if they win events. They compete simply for the honor of their country and the sport.

Mestizos are people who have both American Indian and European backgrounds. Such native peoples and mestizos were the first real cowboys, or vaqueros.

39

Handling a lasso is an important skill in the Mexican rodeo. Steeped in the traditions of the 19th century, the rodeo remains a popular form of entertainment in Mexico today.

Many charros grow up around the charrería lifestyle. As children, they often lived on ranches and followed in the bootsteps of their family members. They are often passionate about their vocation, since it is a family tradition handed down from generation to generation.

Music played by a *mariachi* band usually marks the beginning of the charrería. Members of horseman groups tend to march in front of the crowd first. The state charro association president comes out next. Then team

Women can participate in charrerías too. They can ride in the escaramuza event, which was begun in the 1950s.

members of opposing teams appear. Some of these people walk, ride horses, or wave banners in support of the sport. After this mini-parade, the competition begins.

Similar to the American rodeo, the charerría has a series of separate events that determine the overall winner. Scores are given based on how well the horse responds to the rider's orders. Competitors are judged for style as well as execution. The *cala de caballo* involves a horse and rider. The charro must make the horse follow a specific course that may include many twists and turns. The horse even has to be led backward. This event measures the handler's skill as well as the horse's training. Next comes the *piales al lienzo* (lassos in the curtain). The object is to rope a horse's or bull's hind legs as it gallops past. The *coleadero* is the third part of the sport. The successful entrant rides a horse alongside a bull. He must then pull the bull's tail while turning quickly. This action is supposed to make the bull do a somersault and land on its back. *Jineteo de toros* is bullback riding, while *jineteo de equinos* is horseback riding. In both events, the charro rides the animal until it stops trying to knock him off. *La terna* is next, requiring that a calf be lassoed. The winners are the team who ropes the animal the fastest. Contestants then ride half-wild horses, called broncos. The *piales* and *manganas* require that horsemen rope all four of a horse's legs to make it stop running. The final contest is called the *paso de la muerte*—the death pass. A horseback rider must jump on top of a bronco. He is not to get off the horse until the bucking stops.

Like the bullfight, the charrería is a distinctive part of Mexican culture.

TEXT-DEPENDENT QUESTIONS

In what Mexican state did the charrería (Mexican rodeo) originate during the 19th century? What sort of music is played at the start of a charrería?

RESEARCH PROJECT

Using the Internet or your school library for research, write a one-page report describing the differences between the charrería and an American rodeo today.

 WORDS TO UNDERSTAND

goalie—the player who guards the goal in soccer to prevent the opposite team from scoring.

granite—a hard, igneous rock.

Mexicans have been playing ball games for thousands of years. These are the ruins of an ancient ball court at Monte Alban in Oaxaca. The players would move the ball down the court by bouncing it off the stone walls, using their hips.

MEXICANS HOLD THE BALL IN THEIR COURT:
HANDBALL, TENNIS, AND JAI ALAI

Sports that revolve around balls were played by ancient Mexicans. The balls they played with were made of rubber, a material not available in Europe. When the Spaniards came to the New World, they had never seen anything like rubber. They were fascinated with it. Over time, Europeans added the native games to their own culture—and they developed new sports that took advantage of this bouncy material.

One of the ancient games was handball, a sport Mexicans still enjoy today. Throughout the country, Mexicans play different variations of their ancestors' sport. In some areas like Oaxaca and Sinaloa, no courts are needed, and people play handball in open spaces. The Chichimeca

 Aztecs built their main ball court, called a tlachco, in a sacred area. This place was in the middle of Tenochtitlán, their capital city.

44

Handball is an intense game that has caught on in Mexico and around the world. The game requires great mental and physical control.

people were some of the first people to play handball using only one wall. Now, some Mexicans still participate in one-wall handball.

For team handball players, the object of the game is to score the most goals. Players use their hands to make the ball go into the goal. The ball must remain in motion, so people dribble the ball, like in basketball. Any part of the body above the knee can be used to score goals, but kicking the ball is reserved for *goalies* alone. Goals can be quite large, ranging from about six to eight feet high and as wide as 24 feet.

A game that's similar to handball is jai alai. This sport is considered to be the fastest ballgame because the ball is hurled through air at speeds of 188 miles per hour. The game began four centuries ago simply by throwing a ball against a church wall, an activity that was first developed in Spain's Basque region. People came to celebrations in this area to see jai alai games. Translated

CIVILIZATIONS OF THE PAST HAD GLORY DAYS TOO

In Mexico, the Olmec, Maya, and Aztec civilizations played their own unique sports long before the Europeans came. We know this because statues from this time period show men playing sports. Some figures look like today's baseball umpires, as they are clad with masks and padding.

An ancestor of handball probably comes from the ancient Maya. The game they played was pok-a-tok, a combination of soccer, basketball, racquetball, and volleyball. Players wore padded clothing to prevent injuries. Many wore headpieces like those of warriors and hunters. The main object of the game was to get the ball in a stone hoop (pictured). These could be nearly three times as tall as today's basketball hoops! Players also had to keep the ball moving without using their hands. The Aztecs played a similar game called tlachtli.

The games played by these Native Americans did not follow the rules of today's friendly competitions. Instead, a game could be played by feuding regions to avoid war. Many times this handball-like sport became a ritual that crowds came to watch. Losing teams were often sacrificed. Mayan priests took the severed heads of sacrificial victims and bounced them down temple staircases as if they were balls!

Arturo Rosas of Mexico's national handball team takes a shot in a 2007 match against Argentina.

from the Basque word, *jai alai* means "merry festival." When the Spaniards came to Mexico, they found the natives there already playing their own form of handball, and today's jai alai soon evolved.

Mexicans played jai alai years before a court was built just for the sport, but in 1928, doors opened to Mexico's first jai alai court, built in Mexico City. Now cities like Acapulco, Tijuana, and Cancún have jai alai facilities. Both Mexicans and tourists come to see the exciting sport.

The game's unique equipment sets jai alai apart from any other sport. In other games, substitutions can be made when an item is missing, but this would not work in jai alai. For example, if a goal is missing from a soccer field it can be replaced with some wire and netting. But in jai alai, the tools are very special and hard to replicate. Necessary tools include:

* The ball, or *pelota*. No other sport uses a harder ball. It is a little smaller than a baseball and harder than a baseball bat. Inside the ball is a pure form of Brazilian rubber. Nylon coats this rubber. The outside of the ball is made of goatskin. Balls tend to have short life spans because of the force that hits them. Goatskin wraps may come apart just 20 minutes after the start of a game. So extra balls are needed for continued play.

* The basket, called the *cesta*. This piece of equipment is essential to the game of jai alai. Players strap this hand-shaped basket to their wrists so they can throw the ball and catch it. The cesta is made of wicker. Players are often fitted so their cestas can be handmade just for them. The wicker basket is made from reeds found exclusively in the Pyrenees Mountains, and the frame is made of steam-bent chestnut.

* The court, called the *cancha*. This is no ordinary racquetball court. The driving force and impact of the pelota could crumble regular walls, so builders make the cancha's three walls out of **granite**. Even the mighty pelota cannot tear down these strong walls of rock. The court's size can vary, but if you cut an American football field in half, then built 40-foot walls on three sides and see-through wiring on the fourth side, you'd have something about the size of most canchas.

Most of the time, eight teams play jai alai. Every time a team bounces the ball out of bounds or fails to catch the ball in the cesta, the other team scores a point. If a team cannot catch the ball after only one bounce, then the other

47

48

Mexican tennis player Santiago González serves during a 2012 match in the U.S. Open. González is considered to be one of the best doubles tennis players in the world.

team also gains a point. If a player does not return the ball fast enough, the other team again gets a point. In round one, the first team plays the second team. Whoever wins this match plays the third team. The losing team stands at the back of the line for their next turn to play. The point value jumps to two when the second round begins. In most games, the team who earns seven points first is declared the winner.

The object of jai alai is to hurl a ball against the front wall as close to the side wall of the court with so much speed and spin that the opposition cannot catch or return it on the fly or the first bounce. Like tennis, the game starts with a serve. The ball can only bounce one time on the floor before being caught. The teams continue catching the ball and throwing it back to one another, and the ball must remain in motion. Judges keep constant watch to see if a player fails to catch the ball or throws it out of bounds.

Due to the fast-paced and dangerous nature of the game, jai alai can be tough. It can take years of training and practice to succeed in the sport. But couch potatoes can enjoy this exciting sport too. Many canchas are built for spectators who come to watch and wager. Gamblers can win money guessing which team will come in first or second.

Although tennis seems far tamer by comparison, this sport also continues to gain fans in Mexico. While most people watch rather than play, tennis courts can be found in different parts of the country. Tournaments like the Mexican Tennis Open draw international attention. But the equipment and training needed to play can be expensive. For this reason, not every Mexican can afford what it takes to become a true tennis enthusiast.

 TEXT-DEPENDENT QUESTIONS
What was an Aztec ball court called?
In what area was the game of jai alai originally developed?

 RESEARCH PROJECT
Watch the 15-minute-long video "This is Jai Alai" on YouTube at
https://www.youtube.com/watch?v=TgAAcB5erSk.

WORDS TO UNDERSTAND

loincloth—a one-piece garment, often held in place with a belt, that covers a person's genitals and buttocks.

racewalking—a long-distance race that is different from running in that one of the walkers' feet must appear to be in contact with the ground at all times.

Lorena Ochoa is considered to be the greatest Mexican golfer of all time. She was ranked as the world's top female golfer from 2007 until her retirement in 2010. She won 27 times on the LPGA Tour.

MEXICANS SALUTE SOLO SPORTS

Sports in which individuals compete are popular in Mexico. Track and field activities like running and *racewalking* interest many people. Lifting weights is another way to work out alone, and Mexicans are also discovering the advantages of golf. Ring sports like boxing are found throughout the countryside and draw many crowds. Cycling both on tracks and off-road terrain make bicycles a common choice for sports fans.

Jogging and running are of interest to many Mexicans. Both cross-country running and sprinting offer a challenging workout. The natural beauty of Mexico's coastlines, mountains, and canyons make even the most routine run refreshing for body, mind, and soul. Mexican track meets and races are not common, however. Many Mexican runners practice in their homeland but enter international events. In recent Olympics, runners like Ana Guevara, Adriana Fernández, and Alejandro Cárdenas have represented Mexico. During the 2004 Olympics in Athens, Greece, Ana Guevara won a silver medal for the 400-meter running event.

The marathon demands that entrants be in great shape. This event consists of

52

Alejandro Cárdenas lifts up his bronze medal to photographers after winning the 400 meter sprint. Mexican runners have been very successful in international competitions.

running 26.2 miles. Gérman Silva finished a respectable fifth place in the 1996 Olympics. To train for such a run, he and other top Mexican runners train at Nevado de Toluca, where the volcano called Xinantécatl churns out champions. This Mexican landmark towers at 15,387 feet (4,663 meters). At the top, temperatures are well below freezing. At the base, desert-like conditions make the air scorchingly hot. Because it requires more effort to breathe, running at such high altitudes strengthens lungs, while the high temperatures at the volcano's base help build endurance. While he was training, Silva lived in a hostel at 12,300 feet. He conditioned his body by making it adjust to such a change in altitude. His shelter did not even have heat, water, or electricity. He traded showers and hot meals for the sheer love of running.

SORAYA JIMÉNEZ MENDÍVIL

The 2000 Olympics in Sydney, Australia, were exciting for Mexico. On September 18, an unforgettable event occurred: Soraya Jiménez became the first woman to win a gold medal for Mexico. She earned the only gold medal ever won for weightlifting in her country. This was the first gold medal for Mexico since the 1984 games in Los Angeles, and Jiménez was the first woman to ever win a medal in weightlifting for Mexico.

At the age of 23, Jiménez won the 58-kilogram weightlifting category. She measured only five feet tall and weighed in at 128 pounds—but the stocky athlete lifted an amazing 281 pounds for the win. How could she manage such a feat? "All I can say is practice," Jiménez said. "You never know what you might do." Jiménez, who hails from a Mexico City suburb, also studied law before achieving Olympic stardom. In her spare time she enjoys basketball and badminton.

Her victory in Sydney inspired many young women in Mexico. One was María Espinoza, who at the 2008 Olympics became the second Mexican woman to win a gold medal in an individual event (taekwondo). Espinoza returned to the Olympics in 2012 and won a bronze medal.

53

A Tarahumara Indian runs in a footrace that is part of the Feast of San Lorenzo celebration. Running is viewed by Mexican tribes not only as exercise but as recreation also.

Running is nothing new for a breed of Mexicans called the Tarahumaras. Their real name is *Rarámuri*, which means "the people who are light of foot." They are probably the purest Indians that still exist in Mexico. The Tarahumaras consider running part of their civilization. These people practice their basic belief of living in harmony with both nature and neighbors. Today, many still wear traditional clothing. Men wear **loincloths** and baggy cotton shirts. Women wear skirts and a loosely fitted cotton blouses. And everyone wears headbands.

In earlier times, the Tarahumaras ran long distances through the countryside. But new developments and construction have forced them into a remote area. They now live in the Sierra Tarahumara, an area of Chihuahua high above sea level. Through the years, their lungs have adjusted to the high altitude and become stronger because of it. This added lungpower makes these runners hard to beat.

Tarahumaras love to eat and run. They created their own version of fast food years ago when they ran so swiftly they would actually chase down their dinner! Deer and mountain goats could not outrun them. Today, Tarahumaras run relays without stopping. Some of these races can exceed 230 miles.

Bicycling is another recreation Mexicans enjoy, but in some areas of Mexico, bicycles are not seen as sports equipment but as transportation. In bigger cities, people use bicycles to get around town and avoid traffic. But recreational cycling draws Mexican fans. In more populated areas, like Mexico City, cyclists can use tracks. Mountain bikers can explore Mexico's majestic backcountry. Chihuahua's colorful Copper Canyon and the great, green gorges of the Sierra Madre mountains offer cyclists adventure. Every year, cyclists can compete in a variety of tournaments sponsored in Mexico. In the 2004 Athens

55

For nearly 20 years, Julio César Chávez dominated the welterweight boxing class. He retired with a record of 103-5-2, including 86 wins by knockout.

Olympics, Mexico's Belem Guerrero Méndez earned a silver medal in women's cycling, raising the country's interest in the competitive sport.

Individual contact sports are also popular in Mexico. Several top boxers have come from Mexico, including Julio César Chávez. Cities may host boxing tournaments, but even in remote areas, villagers practice their boxing techniques. Some of these events may be in fields and can draw a crowd. Mexicans call wrestling *luche libre*, or free fight. Spectators can buy tickets to watch this form of international wrestling.

Golfing appeals to Mexicans who enjoy solo sports, and golfers are finding more and more areas to play throughout the country. Guadalajara is considered the golf capital of Mexico. This city has about six different courses that are nice enough for champions to putt on. Golf used to be just for the very rich, but as more courses are built and the sport gains more fans, greater numbers of Mexicans have the opportunity to tee off.

One athlete, Lorena Ochoa, helped to put golf in the spotlight throughout Mexico. Born in 1981 in Guadalajara, Ochoa began her competitive golf career in college. In 2001, she became the youngest winner of Mexico's National Sports Award. She joined the LPGA Tour—the world's most prestigious golf league for women—in 2003, and was named Rookie of the Year in her first season. By 2007, she was the top-ranked female golfer in the world. She held this ranking until 2010, when she decided to retire from the sport. By that point Ochoa already had won 27 tournaments, more than enough to be admitted into the World Golf Hall of Fame.

Whether their games are ancient or new, solo or team, Mexicans love to play. In short, the sports of Mexico are as diverse as the country itself.

TEXT-DEPENDENT QUESTIONS

What Amerindian tribe native to Mexico is famous for long-distance running?

What Olympic cyclist helped to raise interest in the sport with her 2004 victory?

RESEARCH PROJECT

The Olympic Games are the most prestigious international athletic competition. Summer and winter Olympic games are held every four years, and draw the top amateur athletes from around the world. Go to the International Olympic Committee's official website (http://www.olympic.org/ioc) and find a list of events. Choose one event that interests you, and use your school library or the Internet to do some research about it. Write a report explaining how athletes train for this event, and what special abilities or skills are required. Mention some of the best athletes to have competed in this event, and how they did. Include the current Olympic and world records for this event, if applicable.

SERIES GLOSSARY

adobe—a building material made of mud and straw.

Amerindian—a term for the indigenous peoples of North and South America before the arrival of Europeans in the late 15th century.

conquistador—any one of the Spanish leaders of the conquest of the Americas in the 1500s.

criollo—a resident of New Spain who was born in North America to parents of Spanish ancestry. In the social order of New Spain, criollos ranked above mestizos.

fiesta—a Mexican party or celebration.

haciendas—large Mexican ranches.

maquiladoras—factories created to attract foreign business to Mexico by allowing them to do business cheaply.

mariachi—a Mexican street band that performs a distinctive type of music utilizing guitars, violins, and trumpets.

Mesoamerica—the region of southern North America that was inhabited before the arrival of the Spaniards.

mestizo—a person of mixed Amerindian and European (typically Spanish) descent.

Nahuatl—the ancient language spoken by the Aztecs; still spoken by many modern Mexicans.

New Spain—name for the Spanish colony that included modern-day Mexico. This vast area of North America was conquered by Spain in the 1500s and ruled by the Spanish until 1821.

plaza—the central open square at the center of Spanish cities in Mexico.

pre-Columbian—referring to a time before the 1490s, when Christopher Columbus landed in the Americas.

FURTHER READING

Gatch, Tom. *Hooked on Baja: Where and How to Fish Mexico's Legendary Waters.* East Yorkshire, UK: Countryman, 2007.

Goldblatt, David. *The Ball Is Round: A Global History of Soccer.* New York: Riverhead Books, 2008.

Gritzner, Charles F. *Mexico.* New York: Chelsea House, 2012.

Kent, Deborah. *Mexico.* New York: Children's Press, 2012.

McDougall, Christopher. *Born to Run: A Hidden Tribe, Superathletes, and the Greatest Race the World Has Never Seen.* New York: Vintage, 2011.

Valay, Ana Patricia. *Giovani dos Santos.* Philadelphia: Mason Crest, 2013.

Vazquez-Lozano, Gustavo. *Javier "Chicharito" Hernandez.* Philadelphia: Mason Crest, 2013.

Wallechinsky, David, and Jaime Loucky. *The Complete Book of the Olympics.* London: Aurum Press, 2014.

INTERNET RESOURCES

Futbol in Mexico
http://www.fifa.com
http://www.concacaf.com
http://www.femexfut.org.mx

Mexican League baseball
http://www.milb.com/index.jsp?sid=l125

Mexicans in Major League Baseball
http://www.baseball-reference.com/bio/Mexico_born.shtml

Charrería
https://www.tshaonline.org/handbook/online/articles/llc04
http://theautry.org/explore/exhibits/charreria.html

Handball
http://www.ihf.info

Bullfighting
http://www.bullfights.org

Golf
http://www.lorenaochoa.com
http://www.pgatour.com/players/player.02213.lee-trevino.html

Mexican star Giovani dos Santos (right) fights for control of the ball during a match with the national team against New Zealand.

INDEX

PICTURE CREDITS

ABOUT THE AUTHOR

Erica M. Stokes is a freelance writer. Her work for children and young adults has been published in magazines, Web sites, software, and books. She currently resides in the Tennessee Valley of northern Alabama.